BUT I'LL BE BACK AGAIN

And then there was Calvin Ramsey, who one night took it upon himself to tell me everything my mother had left out when she gave me the how-babies-are-made talk. Calvin was the wildest boy I knew, and also one of the nicest. The whole town liked him, though most folks would have locked up their young girls if they'd known what he was telling us. I don't know where Calvin got his information on men and women, but one evening he sat on my front porch until seven o'clock the next morning describing all the parts my mother had forgotten to mention. It was one of my mother's finest traits that she trusted me to stay on that front porch all night long, and this was convenient, because when Calvin started talking to me and to our friend Mike Halstead, who had also stopped by, nothing less than a bomb could have moved me.

BUT I'LL BE BACK AGAIN

OTHER BOOKS BY CYNTHIA RYLANT INCLUDE

A Blue-Eyed Daisy
Children of Christmas
Every Living Thing
A Fine White Dust
A Kindness
Missing May
Soda Jerk
Waiting to Waltz

Cynthia Rylant

BUT
I'LL BE
BACK
AGAIN

A Beech Tree Paperback Book
New York

First Beech Tree Edition, 1993.
Published by arrangement with Orchard Books, a division of Franklin Watts.
10 9 8 7 6 5 4 3 2 1

Printed in the United States of America

"I'll Be back," © 1964 Northern Songs Limited; "It's Only Love," © 1965
Northern Songs Limited; "Revolution," © 1968 Northern Songs Limited;
"I'm Looking Through you," © 1965 Northern Songs Limited; "Can't Buy
Me Love," © 1964 Northern Songs Limited; "Baby's in Black," © 1964
Northern Songs Limited; "In My Life," © 1965 Northern Songs Limited:
All songs by John Lennon and Paul McCartney. All rights Controlled and
Administered by MCA MUSIC PUBLISHING, A Division of MCA INC.,
New York, NY 10019. Under license from ATV MUSIC. ALL RIGHTS
RESERVED. USED BY PERMISSION. Photo of Robert F. Kennedy
courtesy of The John Fitzgerald Kennedy Library. Photo of the Beatles
courtesy of The Picture Collection, The Branch Libraries, The New York
Public Library. Photos on pages 65 and 78 by Jon Harper.
Library of Congress Cataloging-in-Publication Data
Rylant, Cynthia.
But I'll be back again : an album / Cynthia Rylant.
p.   cm.
"A Richard Jackson book."
Summary: The author relates her experiences
growing up in a small West Virginia town.
ISBN 0-688-12653-7
1. Rylant, Cynthia—Biography—Youth—Juvenile literature.
2. Authors, American—20th century—Biography—Juvenile literature.
3. West Virginia—Social life and customs—Juvenile literature.
[1. Rylant, Cynthia—Childhood and youth.   2. Authors, American.]   I. Title.
PS3568.Y55Z464   1993   813'.54—dc20
93-16188   CIP   AC

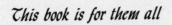

This book is for them all

BUT I'LL BE BACK AGAIN

You know, if you break my heart
I'll go,
But I'll be back again.
'Cause I
Told you once before goodbye,
But I came back again.

I'll Be Back
JOHN LENNON AND PAUL McCARTNEY

*I*F you are a child who is never told the truth, you begin to make up your own. After my father left, and no one mentioned his name again, I simply made things up about him. When the teacher in fourth grade asked me where he was, I said he was in San Francisco on business. He had been gone since I was four, so I guess I could have said he'd been in San Francisco on business for five years. But, of course, San Francisco was just another invention of mine, trying to make a father for myself out of nothing. I had no idea where he was or what he was doing.

They say that to be a writer you must first have an unhappy childhood. I don't know if unhappiness is necessary, but I think maybe some children who have suffered a loss too great for words grow up into writers who are always trying to find those words, trying to find a meaning for the way they have lived. Painters do that. And composers. Everything they have lived is squeezed onto canvas or is penned between the bars of a page of music. It is as if we, as children, just *felt* the life, then after we grew up we wanted to *see* it. So we create stories and paintings and music, not so much for the world as for ourselves.

When I was four I lost both my parents. What happened before that I don't much remember. I can tell you only that my father was an alcoholic and I felt a lot of unhappiness when I was with my parents in those very early years. I think I believed that if I were really really good then I would make them happy and they wouldn't fight. Children always think they can make their parents happy, so they try a hundred different ways to please them, but nothing works. The parents still yell at each other and they still yell at their children, and all the goodness in the world, or in one little child, will not help that. No one ever told me when I was little that my parents' battles were not my fault. I am certain I must have felt they were, and I believe I grew up with this big feeling inside that said, "Whenever anyone who is with you is unhappy, it is your fault." I didn't know, growing up, that I didn't have to make people happy.

I lost my parents when my mother finally left my father and his alcohol, bundling me onto an airplane and flying from Illinois to my grandparents' house in West Virginia. My father was a soldier who had been in the Korean War, and as we flew away from him he was dying. In Korea he had contracted a serious disease called hepatitis, which nearly killed him. After the war he was still weak, and maybe if he had stopped drinking he would have become stronger and healthier and lived to see me grow up into a writer. But he could not stop drinking, and with every beer, with every glass of whiskey, he died a little more. After I flew away from him that day I would not see him again, because he would spend the next eight years away from me getting sicker and sicker until he was gone.

I did not have a chance to know him or to say goodbye to him, and that is all the loss I needed to become a writer.

My mother and I flew to my grandparents' house, then after a few months, she left. She needed training for a job so she would be able to work and raise me by herself. She decided to become a nurse. She went away to nursing school and left me behind, four and a half years old, in my grandparents' small white house in southern West Virginia. She would be away nearly four years.

My mother wrote to me regularly (putting a stick of chewing gum inside every letter), and a few times a year she was able to come and see me. But it was not enough for a little girl. I believe that deep down I felt I just had not been good enough to make her want to stay. For a child there is never a good reason for a mother to leave. My mother's few trips each year to see me, instead of making things better, only made things worse. It would be wonderful having her back with me again, and I would have so much to tell her and so many things to show her. Then suddenly it would be time for her to go, and I could hardly bear it. I·lay in my grandparents' bed and cried in agony as everyone stood in the driveway, saying goodbye to my mother as she got in the car. I would lie in that bed and cry all the tears a little girl could possibly cry. Then finally I would dry my eyes, and I would not cry so hard again until my mother's next visit.

Luckily, though, in that small white house lived those who

could help me heal. I had two uncles and two aunts and two cousins and two grandparents . . . and they all loved me.

Uncle Joe was my hero because he was handsome and the best basketball player at Shady Spring High School. He used to tell me that I wasn't born like regular babies but that someone had found me under a rock in the hog lot. When I was twelve years old I watched him leave on a plane to fight in the Vietnam War. And many years later, in my first novel, *A Blue-Eyed Daisy*, I wrote a chapter for him, a chapter about an uncle who is a soldier and a hero.

My Aunt Sue was in high school, too, and she let me sleep with her. When she said funny things in bed that made me giggle, she'd say my giggle box was turned over. I'd lie in bed giggling uncontrollably, believing that this little silver box in my stomach, like a music box, was turned over on its head.

Also in that white house sometimes was my Uncle Dean, who had joined the Navy. When he was home on leave he would look at me with kind crinkly eyes and in that tough-guy way of his tell me I was a fart-blossom because I wasn't big enough to be a poot-bloom.

When my pretty Aunt Dot was home from South Carolina, she bought me things and called me Lucy Kate, the nickname my mother often used for me. I called her Auntie Dotty.

My cousins Peter and Betty were also living with my grandparents because their mother and father had gone to Alaska for a year with the Air Force. Peter was a year older than I and Betty was two years older.

My cousins and I were always in trouble. One day when we were playing hide-and-seek and Betty was It, Peter and I hid together in the johnny-house. When my grandmama discovered we were in there (Betty had given up hunting and gone to her for help), she came after us with the switch. A boy and a girl hiding together in a johnny-house—even if they *were* first cousins—was improper and outrageous and she left a few red switch marks on our legs to teach us so. Never again did it cross my mind to hide in a toilet with a boy.

But despite the switchings now and then, my grandmother was a gentle woman, and it was in her love and safety, and the kind presence of my grandfather, that I managed to survive the loss of my dear parents.

We had no running water in our house—all of our water was carried from the well in buckets—so baths were either taken in large metal tubs or simply by washing off in the kitchen. My grandmother would set me, Peter, and Betty naked on the kitchen counter and with a pan of water and a soapy cloth work over the three of us at once. Since we spent a lot of time in the woods, we were prone to picking up ticks, and during these washings my grandmother would find them on us, sometimes in the strangest, most unmentionable places. You can't just pull a tick off, because he latches onto you with these little hook-legs. So we got them off by holding the burning end of a cigarette to their backs, which would make any bug jump. I don't need to tell you what it's like to see a hot cigarette coming toward your skin like that, particularly in an unmentionable place.

The days in that house were peaceful and comforting to me. We had little money, especially after my grandfather was hurt in the coal mine and couldn't work anymore—and there were all of our mouths to feed. But we were never hungry, and I had an imagination that took the place of books we couldn't buy and television shows we couldn't pick up.

The only time I remember any disappointment in having no money was the Christmas my grandparents took me into town to get a toy at a place for needy children. We went into an auditorium. The toys children could choose from were spread out on a big stage and everyone had to sit and wait his turn to go up and get one. Right away I spotted a nurse kit and longed desperately to have it, mostly because of my absent mother. But by the time I reached my turn on the stage, the kit had been taken. I don't remember what toy I finally did choose, but whatever it was, it did not take away the aching for that nurse kit. The memory of that wanting was so strong in me that when I grew up, I wrote a story about a poor boy who wants a toy doctor kit for Christmas. Year after year he hopes for a doctor kit, and year after year it never comes. But when he grows up, he finally gets one, because he becomes a real doctor. Writing stories has given me the power to change things I could not change as a child. I can make boys into doctors. I can make fathers stop drinking. I can make mothers stay.

My years with my grandparents were good ones, and while I waited for both my father and my mother to come back, I had big stacks of pancakes and hot cocoa, hound dogs and chickens, teaberry leaves and honeysuckle, and aunts and cousins to sleep with at night and hug until someone could return for me.

It's only love, and that is all,
Why should I feel the way I do?
It's only love, and that is all,
But it's so hard loving you.

It's Only Love
JOHN LENNON AND PAUL McCARTNEY

$\mathcal{M}$Y favorite toy when I was very young and still living with my parents was a stuffed monkey wearing white plastic shoes, whom I named Jo-Jo. He disappeared sometime after I was separated from my father, and in a weird way I searched for both of them for years. When my father died, I stopped looking for him, but I have not given up on Jo-Jo.

My mother became a nurse, and when I was eight I left my grandparents' country house to live with her in a little nearby town called Beaver. We found an apartment in a house which was split down the middle. The left side was ours. For the first time I had an indoor toilet, and during that first week in the apartment, peeing was just about the most exciting thing in my life.

Beaver was full of kids, mostly boys, one of whom lived in the right side of my house. He was two years older than I and at first he avoided me like the measles. But there is no way two kids living with only a thin wall between them can stay strangers. I heard every fight he had with his big sister, knew every time he was in trouble with his dad. Nothing was a secret from me, and being no fool he became my friend. His name was Ronnie Morris.

On Friday nights I went into Ronnie's side of the house to eat popcorn with his family and watch movies on TV. All of us were in some sort of pajamas, drinking red Kool-Aid, passing around a big plastic bowl, and it never occurred to me that this was odd, that there was probably no other boy and girl in our entire school who visited with each other in their pajamas.

Over the years, Ronnie and I watched each other grow and change and look for romance. It was hard looking for romance when the boy next door kept reminding me of the way my bathing suit hiked up my behind and showed everything, or of the fact that my underarms were hairier than his. I could retaliate by pointing out that, since he was putting on weight, he needed a bra even more than I did, and that would shut him up a while. Once, to make a girl he liked jealous, he asked me to kiss him while she was looking. I did, and we both nearly threw up.

But that all came later. When we met, I was entering third grade and learning to live with a mother I was thrilled to have again but whom I really did not know.

I don't know why people say children do not fall in love until they have hair on all the important parts of their bodies and know how to shave it off. In first grade James Miller was wildly in love with me and remained that way for twelve years. He also loved Christy Sanders, but then, he was an open-minded boy so why shouldn't he? When I changed schools in third grade (leaving a broken-hearted James behind until junior high), a boy named Jerry Redding fell in love with me on my first day and made the mistake of admitting it to some-one. At recess he found himself screaming for mercy as he was pinned to a brick wall by eight boys while a group of girls led me to him. It was not exactly a heart-stopping intro-duction, and Jerry did not look me in the eye during that entire year without blushing.

Some say that girls begin looking for love much earlier than boys, but I think none of the girls take it that seriously. I think that boys, on the other hand, seem not to go looking for romance at all but instead fall into it like some gaping pit. While the girls are passing notes on who the object of their latest crush is, boys are just gazing about like water oxen when, *bam*: they see a face and they're hooked for the next hundred years.

When the Beatles came to America in 1964, the boys lost most of us girls to either John Lennon, Paul McCartney, George Harrison, or Ringo Starr (not many to Ringo) and watched in total disgust as all of us became sick with love for twenty-year-old men in matching suits. There is no love quite so pure and wonderful as the love you feel for somebody you don't know one thing about. I fell in love with Paul.

In my little West Virginia town I dreamed that, of all the girls in the world, I would be the one Paul McCartney would eventually find happiness with. I kept his picture beside my bed and on my four walls. I wore Beatles scarves, necklaces, bracelets, and badges. I stood in line for two hours at the movie theater to see the Beatles' first film, *A Hard Day's Night*, and when I got inside all I did was yell and cry with the rest of the girls who yelled and cried. I was only ten years old, but I might as well have been Juliet crying out for her Romeo, so enormous was my love and so great my pain. After the movie we all went to the Tip Top restaurant for banana splits, and within seconds we were back to talking about clothes and boys, and no one would have guessed what a bunch of lunatics we'd been just minutes before.

I think that in a lot of ways Paul McCartney became for me my lost father and my lost Jo-Jo monkey. When my mother went off to nursing school, no one ever spoke of my father and eventually I became ashamed to ask about him. He wrote a few letters to me those first months I lived with my grandparents, but soon the letters stopped and no one talked, and no one would talk about him until I was nine and my mother mentioned that he was living in Florida and they were getting an official divorce.

What I have found out since I grew up is that no one in my family knew where my father was for nearly three years after my mother and I left Illinois on the plane. And since the truth might have made him look bad, they had decided not to speak of him at all. It is an unfortunate thing grown-ups do sometimes: if the truth is bad, they don't tell their children anything. And even if they don't know the truth, they still remain silent and their children have to imagine all the things that could be wrong. Children always imagine the worst, because they have so much to lose.

The memory of my father grew dimmer and dimmer as I grew, and what was left was a strong feeling that I could not ask to know anything about anyone, that I must wait to be told the truth instead of pursuing it myself. When I was grown up I had to learn all over again how to be honest and how to expect that from others, and how to find out the truth instead of always guessing at it.

So Paul and the Beatles became more for me than just rock 'n' roll heroes. They became something for me to know, a dream I could see each time I opened a package of Beatles bubble-gum cards or watched them on TV or bought their latest record. For all their distance and their difference, I felt I knew them better than the father I could not find and the mother who did not speak of him.

We all wanted to be rock 'n' roll stars. The boys wanted electric guitars for Christmas. I, too, wanted an electric guitar and one Christmas got a hard plastic one which didn't sound like much but looked great slung across my back as I walked around town. In our small Appalachian living rooms we watched our black-and-white television sets to learn how to dress like rockers. Ponchos were popular, and white boots for girls, called Shindig boots. Most of the boys wanted long hair, but the schools made them get haircuts and the grown-ups all complained about how wild we were getting. There wasn't much danger to our wildness, though. Drugs weren't as common as they are now, and apart from sneaking a drink of beer or blowing hard into a paper bag to pass out (dumb), our wildness was modest at best. For a while some kids were sniffing glue, but when word got out that it would either kill you or send you to an insane asylum, the fad kicked under.

Even when the Beatles themselves rebelled and went off to a guru in India and experimented with drugs and wore the clothing of young revolutionaries, we didn't change that much because about the only place to shop for clothes was Montgomery Ward and drugs were so far away that we still thought the word meant arthritis pills.

In this respect ours was an easier world than today's in which to live out a childhood. But, like you, we still had our bodies to deal with, and our parents, and each other.

You say you want a revolution.
Well, you know
We all want to change the world.

Revolution
JOHN LENNON AND PAUL McCARTNEY

*W*HEN I was in the sixth grade a new boy came to our school. His name was Richard Cole, and he was living with a foster family. With jet black hair, he looked like something out of an Italian spy movie, and I was a goner the minute I saw him.

We began writing love letters to each other in school; I don't know where he got his talent for words, but this boy's letters practically sizzled in my hands. We were in different classrooms and never talked much face to face, but this was fine by me as long as he kept those firecracker messages coming.

Unfortunately, my mother found one of them. She was ready to chain me in the basement for the next ten years or until I gave up Richard, whichever came first. I had never seen her so upset about a boy, and though today I can't remember a thing Richard wrote, I know now it must have been pretty juicy stuff. My mother even threatened to send me to live with my father, which shows how crazy the whole thing had made her.

So, I had to write a goodbye letter to Richard. And goodbye was right on target, it turned out, because shortly after that Richard left town, taking with him my brand-new fancy radio I'd loaned him. My mother's instincts were right: I had been consorting on paper with a criminal. I never heard what happened to Richard after that and actually thought more about my fancy radio than ever I thought about him.

Richard showed up at a bad time anyway, since around then my mother had reluctantly given me the talk all parents dread: how babies are made. I remember she used a little pamphlet to help her through the tough parts, but even with that, all of it sounded pretty unexciting, if not awkward, to me. However, I sat attentively through the speech and even asked a couple of off-the-wall questions I hoped would trip her up (like, can a woman keep her underpants on and still have a baby). But when she told me about girls having menstrual periods, I must have found it so dull that I blocked it out—which was unfortunate because soon after that, remembering her speech would have saved me a lot of pure *terror*.

I spent one Friday night with a girlfriend and when I woke up the next morning I discovered some odd mess in my underpants. I was mortified and didn't even tell my friend; I just hurried home to change, stuffing my dirty underwear in the hamper. But the mess kept reappearing all that day, and finally I decided I was dying, that my insides were caving in and slowly leaking out of me and I wouldn't live to see seventh grade. I could think of no one to tell, so I just suffered through the hours with my heart pounding and my mind praying for a little more time on earth.

Luckily for me it was laundry day, and when my mother

found all my dirty underwear that afternoon, she asked me about my menstrual period starting. I was so embarrassed at my stupidity that I couldn't tell her I'd just spent the day debating whether I wanted to be buried or cremated.

Boys were lucky, I thought. They could grow up in private, but girls had to have all sorts of contraptions which drew attention, including that worst of all, the *bra*.

I hated bras. I'd been an ace volleyball player until I started wearing bras. I could never keep the strap up; sometimes I couldn't even keep a bra in the right place. I'd serve a volleyball and either the strap would be hanging over my elbow or the bra would be up around my neck. Every move I made on that volleyball court was calculated to keep my bra under control, and it cost me a lot of points.

Then there was the hair. I don't know why I got the gene for gorilla hair-growth, but I did and in sixth grade I felt more like Cheetah than Jane. While my girlfriends stayed hairless and smooth, my underarms and legs began to look a lot like their *fathers'* underarms and legs. Because my mother thought I was too young to start shaving, I wore shirts with sleeves and tights on my legs so no one would see I was turning into a man. When Karen Bowman told me her older brother hated hairy women, my shirt sleeves got even longer.

Finally, after a swimming trip during which I refused to play volleyball in the water because I'd have to raise my hairy arms, I began a one-girl revolt in my home. I wanted to shave and I wanted to wear nylon hose and I picketed my mother for these rights. On the walls of our little apartment I posted signs: "I Hate My Mother," "Nylons Now," and other political-type slogans. I went on strike against conversation and refused to talk to her until I got the hair off and the nylons on.

The campaign lasted only a few hours. Living with a radical wore my mother out, and soon I was happily turning into a girl again under the delicate strokes of a double-edge razor.

Sixth grade seemed overall to be the Year of the Body. Not only was my own changing, but it seemed the whole world was suddenly obsessed with the same subject. One day my friend Debby Ellerman took me to the johnny-house her father liked to use (even though they also had an indoor bathroom), and she showed me the pile of dirty books he read while sitting on the hole. We sneaked a few out and read parts of them, and I was shocked beyond belief. I also wanted to read some more, but I was too timid to ask Debby; thus I blew my only chance at extensive outhouse reading.

Debby had always complained about her dad being a "lollygagger." I never asked her to define what a lollygagger was, but after glimpsing his reading tastes, I had a much better idea.

I guess the entire country was thinking about sex. Many people called that time of the 1960s the Sexual Revolution. I wasn't sure exactly what they meant, but I thought maybe it was related to all that hair that was sprouting under my arms.

When I was learning to dance and to go to parties, somebody in some wild place like New York or San Francisco invented a new dance called The Dog, and it eventually found its way into Appalachia and inside the volunteer firehouse in town where kids went for Friday night dances. I stood in the doorway of the firehouse and watched boys and girls do this "dirty dancing," their private parts sort of bumping together to the beat, and was afraid and wonderfully excited at the same time. And though my mother would likely have died beneath the firehouse bell had she seen me, I went in and danced The Dog, too. Only the risk of parachuting out of an airplane when I was twenty-one ever compared with doing The Dog.

And then there was Calvin Ramsey, who one night took it upon himself to tell me everything my mother had left out when she gave me the how-babies-are-made talk. Calvin was the wildest boy I knew, and also one of the nicest. The whole town liked him, though most folks would have locked up their young girls if they'd known what he was telling us. I don't know where Calvin got his information on men and women, but one evening he sat on my front porch until seven o'clock the next morning describing all the parts my mother had forgotten to mention. It was one of my mother's finest traits that she trusted me to stay on that front porch all night long, and this was convenient, because when Calvin started talking to me and to our friend Mike Halstead, who had also stopped by, nothing less than a bomb could have moved me.

But for all his swagger and confidence, Calvin was really just another of the boys who had fallen into that gaping pit of love. In second grade he fell in love with a girl named Dixie

Lilly, and he never ever stopped loving her. The whole school knew Calvin loved Dixie, and Dixie knew it, too, but she didn't love him back. Still, from second grade to twelfth, Calvin devoted his heart to Dixie. When they graduated from high school and she married somebody else, he kept on loving her. And when her marriage failed and she was free again, Calvin was still there with his love. He married her, and they had a little boy.

Children do fall in love. And some of them hang onto that love even as they work their way through a childhood most grown-ups will not take seriously.

I'm looking through you,
Where did you go?
I thought I knew you,
What did I know?
You don't look different
But you have changed,
I'm looking through you,
You're not the same.

I'm Looking Through You
JOHN LENNON AND PAUL McCARTNEY

*P*OOR JESUS. I took advantage of His good graces hundreds of times as a child. When I lived with my grandparents I attended the Missionary Baptist Church out at the end of the road, and it was there that I learned Jesus would forgive all my sins. My best friend Cindy Mills learned it at the same time, and the two of us made fine use of that good news. Each time we lied about something, we'd say to each other, "We'll ask Jesus to forgive us." Each time we disobeyed somebody, we arranged to tell Jesus that very night. We saw the forgiveness of Jesus as an incredible opportunity to do whatever we wanted—as long as we could get away with it in earthly terms.

There was an innocence about our faith in Jesus that I can admire now. It is something children seem most capable of, this belief that there's some love up there somewhere. As I grew older I would become more afraid of what was up there looking down on me, and I would dread that every act of mine involved some kind of sin.

Growing up in the Bible Belt, I heard a lot about bad people dying, then burning forever in hellfire. I don't know why I didn't give it much thought in my early life, but as I grew bolder (and hairier) with each passing year, I found myself leaning into that talk about hellfire and I started to get a little worried. From what the preachers were telling me, there wasn't a bone in my body that wasn't soaked full of sin, and if I didn't get myself saved in church, well, tomorrow I could be struck by lightning and it would just be too late.

I held out as long as I could, dreading the embarrassment of having to walk down the aisle in church and confess to the preacher and to everyone watching that I was an outright unsaved sinner. But finally a preacher got through to me one Sunday, convincing me and the congregation that God gives no second chances to those who don't walk down that aisle (and in fact, He might even cut life a little shorter for them), so I figured the embarrassment was worth avoiding an eternity of torture and walked down the middle of that church to salvation.

I guess now I look back on that Sunday with a sense of having been tricked into something. If you had to scare somebody into loving you, would you think you were loved for who you are? For me it's the same thing with God: Why would He think anybody really loved Him if the only thing that could get somebody headed in His direction was the threat of burning up forever? It took me until I was grown up to realize I'd gone about religion in all the wrong way, and I had to figure God out again. He kept popping into my books: in *Waiting to Waltz* there are three poems about religion (none of them much flattering to Him, I admit). In *A Blue-Eyed Daisy*, a young girl goes looking for His help when she believes her father is dying. And in *A Fine White Dust*, a boy thinks he's found God in the form of a talented charismatic preacher. It's pretty clear to me that God and I are still doing a lot of talking, and probably always will.

I think my idea of heaven when I was a kid was Christy Sanders' home. She lived in a new brick house with carpeting in it and a bar in the kitchen you could eat on and a picture window in the living room. Her dad wore suits and her mother was queen of the P.T.A. Christy's house always smelled like those chocolate-covered marshmallow cookies you can get at the grocery. Everything in it was new and it matched and it worked.

In the apartment my mother and I shared, there were old gas heaters you had to light with a match and which threatened to blow you up every time you did. We didn't have carpet. We had old green and brown linoleum with cigarette burns in it. Every morning there would be at least one spider in the bathtub, and it would take every ounce of nerve I had to look in and check. Once a really big spider crawled out from under our old couch and I was too scared to step on him; instead I dropped a Sears catalog on his head and left it there for a week, just to make sure he was dead.

If you looked out our front window you would have seen Todd's warehouse and junkyard. It was a long metal building enclosed by a high chain-link fence, and on the outside were rusting barrels and parts of bulldozers and all manner of rotten equipment. There was some talk that the ghost of Mr. Todd's old father walked around that warehouse at night, but I was too worried about spiders in my bathtub to give it much thought.

Wanting Christy Sanders' brick house was just a symptom of the overall desire I had for better things. I read a lot of magazines, and I wanted to live in houses with yellow drapes and backyard pools. I was ashamed of where I lived and felt the world would judge me unworthy because of it. I wouldn't even go to the library in the nearby city because I felt so unequal to city kids. Consequently, I lived on comic books for most of my childhood, until I moved into drugstore paperback romances as a teenager.

As long as I stayed in Beaver, I felt I was somebody important. I felt smart and pretty and fun. But as soon as I left town to go anywhere else, my sense of being somebody special evaporated into nothing and I became dull and ugly and poor. This feeling would stick with me for years, and when I went away to college and met students who had grown up in big northern cities and could breeze through the world talking like they owned it, I realized that no matter how much I studied, or how many college degrees I got, there was one thing I might never fully learn: I might never fully learn that it would be all right for me to have a house that smelled like chocolate-covered marshmallow cookies.

One year, the New Orleans Symphony Orchestra came to play in our junior high school gymnasium. What that orchestra was doing in my little town I cannot imagine, for surely they were all fresh out of London and New York and Los Angeles and didn't need any extra publicity in Beaver, West Virginia.

But the visit of that orchestra was something I have never forgotten. I was not familiar with any real sort of culture. No one I knew played classical records. I had never been to a museum of any kind. In fact, it would not be until I went to college in Charleston, West Virginia, that I set foot in a library or art museum.

The New Orleans Symphony was for me like a visit from God Himself, so full of awe and humility was I. We sat on the hard bleachers our bottoms usually warmed for junior varsity games, and we watched these elegant people who seemed long and fluid like birds play their marvelous instruments. Their music bounced off the blue and gold picture of our school tiger on the wall and the time clock and the heavy velvet curtains we used for school plays, and the gym was transformed into a place of wonder for me.

The conductor was a slender, serious man with a large nose and a lot of dark hair swept back from his forehead. I watched him and I wanted to live in his pink house in New Orleans, surrounded by maids carrying iced tea and peanuts, sleeping each night in a white canopy bed, greeting at the door of our home such notable musicians as Elvis Presley, Paul McCartney, and The Monkees.

Watching the conductor and his beautiful orchestra, I felt something in me that wanted more than I had. Wanted to walk among musicians and artists and writers. Wanted a life beyond Saturdays at G. C. Murphy's department store and Sundays with the Baptist Youth Fellowship.

I wanted to be someone else, and that turned out to be

the worst curse and the best gift of my life. I would finish out my childhood forgetting who I really was and what I really thought, and I would listen to other people and repeat their ideas instead of finding my own. That was the curse. The gift was that I would be willing to try to write books when I grew up.

I'll buy you a diamond ring, my friend,
If it makes you feel all right.
I'll get you anything, my friend,
If it makes you feel all right.
'Cause I don't care too much for money.
For money can't buy me love.

Can't Buy Me Love
JOHN LENNON AND PAUL McCARTNEY

J got my first kiss when I was eleven years old, and for the next several years I did so much kissing that I barely had time to take a breath. I loved to kiss, and still do, and apart from going out for ice cream, there are few things as easy and enjoyable.

My first kiss occurred at a party during a game of Spin the Bottle. Months of cheek-kisses at these occasions had taught me not to expect much when I went into the next room with a boy, so I had not prepared myself for the life-changing event that was to come that night.

The boy was Harold Treadway. He was three years older than I, tall, with dark hair and glasses. Not a bad-looking boy, but I'd never paid him much attention.

When Harold spun the Coke bottle and it pointed its nose at me, I giggled and blushed as I always did and went ahead of him into the next room. I was still giggling when I turned around for my cheek-kiss, and found instead that he was coming straight for my mouth like one of those men in the movies. I said no a couple of times (but not too loudly) and pushed him away a couple of times (but not too hard), then I let him do what he was intent on doing.

Boy, could he kiss. He didn't just peck like a rooster and run. He knew how to mush his mouth around for a while, and as this was happening, I thought every organ inside my body was going to take flight. I had never had such feelings. When he finished with that kiss I was shaking all over and was in love.

Harold became my boyfriend, and we spent the next few months kissing like we might die any minute. He was the best person in the world for teaching a girl how to kiss; I have always wanted to thank him for it (and for the kissing chapter I eventually wrote in *A Blue-Eyed Daisy*). My enthusiasm for smooching would bring me some interesting experiences in the coming years.

After Harold, my next boyfriend was Mike Halstead. Harold had moved on to a ninth-grade girl and Mike came along and took his place. Mike and I had sat through Calvin's elaborations on how babies are made that night on the front porch, and you'd think that having shared that, we'd be too embarrassed to go together. But it was as if Calvin was just an unusual movie we'd gone to see which didn't have anything to do with real life. All we wanted to do was kiss.

Late one afternoon Mike and Calvin stopped by my house. Calvin had a leaf project due at school the next day and they wanted me to come collecting leaves with them. Naturally I went, completely forgetting that I was supposed to wash the dishes before my mother came home from work at seven. I went off into the woods with Calvin and Mike, and though it got dark early and we had to use Calvin's flashlight, we managed to gather a fine bunch of leaves and somehow figure out what kind each was.

We walked back to my house about eight. My mother wasn't there, so Calvin went on home and Mike stayed to sit on the edge of the couch and kiss a while. As we were kissing, though, my mother came through the door. Her face was flushed and in her hand was a switch. In a tense voice she reminded me about the dishes I didn't wash and the note I didn't leave telling her where I went. I tried to explain, but she cut me short and told Mike to go home. Poor Mike. I could tell by his eyes that he wanted to pull me out the door with him, that he wanted to save me from the trouble I was in.

He left quietly and then my mother gave me the first switching I'd had in five years. I was twelve years old, and I was humiliated. I soaked in the bathtub afterward, my legs stinging, and we never spoke about that night again.

I understand now that it must have been my new sexuality which frightened my mother. I only had been collecting leaves, but she was a parent watching her daughter change and she probably imagined worse things.

Parents can be forgiven that. They can be forgiven their fears.

In seventh grade a boy named Jimmy Williams got a crush on me. Seventh grade was an exciting, heady time. We were in junior high school at last and we had our own football field and marching band and the fall season was saturated with our tremblings. I was a majorette for the band, which gave me no end of thrill and pleasure, and Jimmy played on the football team, mostly second-string.

I liked Jimmy and we got along grandly, but I wasn't sure I wanted to be his girlfriend, so things between us were pretty casual.

One night, though, we had a football game with an old rival school we'd hated for years. It was a beautiful October night, full of the smell of P.T.A. popcorn and Juicy Fruit and Pepsi all mixed into the pungency of fall leaves and lime on the yard lines.

The evening was perfect. The band played like it never had, not one majorette dropped a baton, not one fight broke out in the stands. And our team won. It was an ecstatic victory for us, and second-string Jimmy had scored one of the touchdowns.

After the game everyone followed our football team across the field and through the gravel parking lot to the boys' locker room behind the gymnasium. It was in that parking lot, in the dark, amid the exultant crowd and the parked cars, that Jimmy found me.

I do not remember what words he said to me, but the feeling of those few moments has never been lost. His face was full of emotion. It may be that was the finest night of his life. He looked at me tenderly, his eyes clear and honest, and he lifted my white-gloved hand to his lips and kissed it. Then he turned and followed his team into the building.

I have had many romantic moments in my life, but those few minutes with Jimmy Williams are the most graceful I ever experienced.

Robert Rufus was a different story entirely.

It was in eighth grade that I succumbed to Robert's charms. If a playboy ever existed in our school, it was he. Courtship was for Robert a fine art, and that excellence eventually got him inducted into his senior class Hall of Fame as "Biggest Flirt."

During the last few months of eighth grade, Robert pursued me with a vigor unequalled in my young life. He said I was "a gem" and he had elaborate plans for our marriage, which he shared with me during long hours on the telephone. Robert was a handsome boy with a strut and a magnetism about him that made you like him even if you didn't like him. (He also had a slight stutter, but who ever noticed?) And it was on the last day of eighth grade, when Robert had decided to get this romance with me underway, that his talents bloomed like roses.

He walked me home after school. Classes ended early that day, so it was about noon when we strolled in the sun to my house. Robert and I had never really been alone together, and now with my mother at work and a summer afternoon lingering ahead of us, it was the perfect time for romance.

Robert was a very witty boy, and cocky (these qualities, plus his basic integrity, inspired me to use him as the character Rufus in *A Fine White Dust*). I think Robert liked me so much because I could match every smart remark he threw my way with an even smarter one. It was my only ammunition with this overpowering boy, and the constant tension between us honed my desperate sarcasm.

We went into my empty house, talking wittily of course,

and sat on the couch together. It was like sitting with Tom Cruise, so strong was Robert's manly aura. We had talked for some time, with quite a bit of space between us, when suddenly he asked if he could kiss me.

Well, would you refuse Tom Cruise?

I said yes and before I could move an inch he had surged across that distance between us and staggered me with the most powerful smooch I had ever experienced. There are really no words to describe it.

However, it is a cinch to describe what happened next: I jumped up and ran crying into the bathroom. Robert came after me with profound apologies and comforted me as I blew my nose into a wad of toilet paper. (It is a wonder my grandmother wasn't right there with her switch as I stood in a toilet with yet another boy, and this one not even related.)

I was never able to tell Robert that it was not the forwardness of his kiss which made me cry, but the power of it which so moved and frightened me.

For the rest of that summer we flirted back and forth, but for reasons I'm not sure of, our romance remained one of jokes and teasings, and we talked it rather than lived it. Something was missing. Perhaps it was for me a sense of safety. Perhaps I was just too afraid of Robert's power. But it was lovely being "a gem" for a while.

Kissing was one of the sweetest parts of growing up, and not since those years have I felt such magic as when it was all so new and so sincere.

Oh, dear, what can I do?
Baby's in black
And I'm feeling blue
Tell me oh,
What can I do?

Baby's in Black
JOHN LENNON AND PAUL McCARTNEY

$\mathcal{T}$HE year I was thirteen turned out to be a time of burials for me. Within its span, I would mourn two lost heroes.

One was Robert F. Kennedy. He was the brother of President John F. Kennedy, who had been assassinated when I was nine. Robert decided to run for president just as I was turning into a teenager and needed someone to believe in.

I cannot tell you what he stood for exactly, because I never really knew. My loyalty to Bobby Kennedy was the same as that which I bestowed upon the conductor of the New Orleans Symphony Orchestra. It was a loyalty which sprang from a dream in me of a deeper life, a more meaningful life. I had used the Beatles, in one way, to create that dream, just as I had used the elegant conductor. Now another had come with the light of something grander about him, and I became a follower of Bobby Kennedy.

I watched him talk on television and I believed in him. I wanted to be one of those people following him from place to place, protecting him, defending him. He had gentle eyes and looked to me like one who could be easily hurt.

Never would I have imagined that Bobby Kennedy would come to my town, my little home in southern West Virginia which drew to it only people passing through to Florida. That he would come to the place I knew, the place in which I felt safe and important, I never envisioned. One conductor was more than I expected and the last hero I figured on seeing in my life. I believed Bobby Kennedy would remain for me only a kind of king in a faraway castle.

But he came.

West Virginia was an important state to him. It was the state which helped his brother John become president, and Bobby came back to it, to us, to ask for help and for votes for himself. He was scheduled to fly into the county airport, which was only five miles away from my home.

I wore my best dress and my best coat and my nicest white shoes, and my mother took me out to that airport two hours early to wait for Bobby Kennedy. I was one of the first people there, so I got right up against the fence which would separate Bobby from his fans. My mother sat in the car, waiting for me, as I waited for him.

The nice white shoes made my feet hurt, and I got a run in my hose almost immediately. And then it began to rain. It rained for two solid hours. Behind me the crowd grew heavier and noisier and pushy. But I had come early, I was in front, and I was not about to move even for a Mack truck.

Bobby landed in a little plane out on the runway. The local TV crews had their lights on him as he walked across the wet asphalt to the fence where hundreds of West Virginians cheered for him. He reached out to shake their hands, and as I saw him moving along the fence to where I stood, I stretched my arm out as far as it would go and prayed that of all the hands around me and encircling my head, it would be mine Bobby Kennedy would take. And just before he turned to leave, he did. He looked at my face, he smiled, and he shook my hand.

I went home that night a satisfied and happy girl, and when two months later Robert Rufus called me before school one morning and said, "Your hero's dead," I sat down on my bed and cried like a baby. Bobby Kennedy was shot in the back of the head.

As if a cruel trick were being played on me, another hero had come into my life that same year, the year I was thirteen, and he, too, left almost as suddenly.

My father, who had lived in Florida for years without ever writing to me, for unexplained reasons began sending me letters. The letters were loving and cheerful, and it was as if he had been away only a few days instead of nine years. He wanted to see me. He talked about flying up to West Virginia, and about flying me down to Florida. We would go to the beach, he said.

Children can forgive their parents almost anything. It is one of those mysteries of life that no matter how badly a parent treats a child, somewhere in that child is a desperate need to forgive, a desperate need to be loved.

I accepted my father back into my life without reservation. I wrote him long letters and sent him photographs. I told my friends that when he came to West Virginia, he would take us all out to a movie or something.

But then, he got sick. My mother told me that he was in the hospital and my trip to Florida would have to wait a while. And on June 16, while I was in West Virginia planning all the things we would do together, he died. He did not say goodbye.

It is hard to lose someone, even harder to lose him twice, and beyond description to lose him without a goodbye either time. If I have any wish for my own life, it is that I will have a chance to say all my goodbyes.

I did not lose any more heroes until I was grown up and had a child of my own. Then, one night in New York City, my old Beatles hero John Lennon was shot down. Those of us who had spent a childhood wearing Beatles badges and crying through the Beatles' movies looked at John's picture on the evening news and with tears in our eyes we wondered what had happened to us all. What had happened to The Dog and the Shindig boots and the Beatles bubble-gum cards. We were grown up, and it was scary.

I still have my plastic Paul McCartney doll. Somehow all the Beatles scarves and necklaces and badges got lost in all the time it took me to move from being a little girl into becoming a woman. But the little plastic Paul doll was saved somehow, and I keep it safe now in a trunk. Maybe in some way, by protecting this doll, I am protecting that part of my childhood which smells like pink powdered bubble gum and Harold Treadway's mouth and Calvin Ramsey's leaf collection and the rain falling on Bobby Kennedy's face.

All these places had their moments
With lovers and friends
I still can recall.
Some are dead and some are living,
In my life, I've loved them all.

In My Life
JOHN LENNON AND PAUL McCARTNEY

I do not know what became of most of the people I grew up with. Had I stayed there in my little town, I could tell you more. But if I had stayed there, I don't think I would have become a writer who one day would tell you something of her childhood. I think I would have become instead whatever kind of person would fit in best with the people back home. I loved many people there in that place of my growing up, and it was always important to me to be someone with whom they felt comfortable. I don't know if they would have been comfortable with me as a writer. Perhaps they would have celebrated me. But I didn't stay to find out.

I can tell you these things:

My next-door neighbor Ronnie Morris got married, inherited his grandmother's house, and now runs a TV cable repair company.

My kissing teacher, Harold Treadway, stayed there, too. He got married and works in a hospital lab.

My first-grade admirer, James Miller, became a policeman, and my third-grade admirer, Jerry Redding, became a teacher. They both stayed.

Debby Ellerman left her lollygagging father and moved to Virginia, smuggling out a few of his books, I hope.

Calvin Ramsey, sex-education teacher of the century, not only married Dixie, he also became a part-time fundamentalist Christian preacher—and I'm not kidding.

Mike Halstead not only stayed in town, he stayed in the same house he grew up in, continuing to live with his grandmother and play Beatles records.

My best friend Cindy Mills got married and moved to Alabama, where I figure Jesus forgives people, too.

Christy Sanders got married and built a brick house next to her parents' marshmallow-cookie brick house.

Jimmy Williams dropped out of high school and joined the air force. He did not kiss my hand goodbye and I do not know what became of him.

Robert Rufus, playboy extraordinaire, became a marine and then a certified public accountant (which takes more brains than I ever knew he had). We ran into each other once, after we had grown up, and I would have been quite willing then (in a nervous sort of way) to try another one of his kisses. But he was engaged to be married and was reserving his Tom Cruise lips for someone else.

My mother moved to Florida as soon as I graduated from high school. I have one parent buried there and another one alive.

I have read that sometimes people who die try to communicate with those they have left behind. I have wondered if my father ever tried to send me a message, but from what I can tell, nothing got through.

However, one day after I was grown up and a writer, I

came across an old clipping of a newspaper article my father had written when he was a soldier and a reporter for an army newspaper. The story was about army dentists, and that's not a subject you can squeeze a lot of excitement from. But my father wrote a fine, fine article, full of life and color and intelligence, and as I read it, I realized that his voice sounded like mine. And that he had not completely left this world because the sound of him was still alive in over twenty children's books written by the daughter he left behind.

I moved from my small town when I graduated from high school. I went to college, and after college I began to write stories for the first time. I mailed them to New York and almost right away they became published. My first book, *When I Was Young in the Mountains*, was dedicated to my grandparents, to thank them for the time I lived with them.

I was married twice before I reached age thirty and am sorry to say that in spite of all that kissing practice, I didn't get either marriage right. Neither lasted very long. It was painful for me to have made two big mistakes like that, and painful for me to have failed in ways other people could see. I hated saying I was "divorced" because the word itself sounds so ugly—not pretty like "moonbeam" or "shy" or "ivy" or "married." I had to work hard not to be ashamed of the word. I had to work hard to learn from these two divorces what I needed to know about myself. And what I mostly found out is, in a way, connected to that marshmallow-cookie brick house. I found out that I really had not expected very much happiness for my life. Children who suffer great loss often grow up believing deep inside that life is supposed to be hard for them. They sometimes don't know how to find comfort and a life that doesn't hurt. Once I learned how to do this, I was able to make better decisions in everything because I carefully chose only those people and places which offered me peacefulness and love. And today I am happy, and I am even living in my own version of a marshmallow-cookie house.

I also had a little boy of my own when I grew up, and having a child helped me understand how scary it is to be somebody's parent, because you're always afraid you might screw things up for him. I would like my son to have an easier childhood than mine.

But every child will have his heartaches. I just hope that along with these each child will have a hero, and music, and at least one kiss he will never forget.

Peoria, Illinois

Dear Cindy,

How is my little girl getting along
these days. Are you being a good girl and helping
Mother like you used to do. And how are all of
the chickens, dogs and cats getting along. I'll
bet they were really glad to see you again.

Donna and Rickey and Kathy and Patty
and all of your other little friends told me to tell
you hello. Sissy has a nice home with Ann
Comiskey and her two little sisters but Sissy still
likes you the best.

Daddy is taking care of your toys and
watches them so they won't get cold. JoJo + Pete
still fight all the time but they're much better
now.

Daddy misses and loves you very much
and I think you're the finest little girl in the world.
I hope we can see each other before long.

Write to me and don't forget to
bow your head when you say the blessing.
I love you to pieces.

—Daddy

'Sure Wish They'd Hurry'

"I sure wish they'd hurry." This could well be the thoughts of pretty little 7-year-old Cynthia as she waits her turn in the toy line at the 32nd annual Mac's Memorial Toy Fund Party Thursday. Some 2.700 children were invited to the party at the Memorial Building.

(Post-Herald Photo by Bedford Morris)

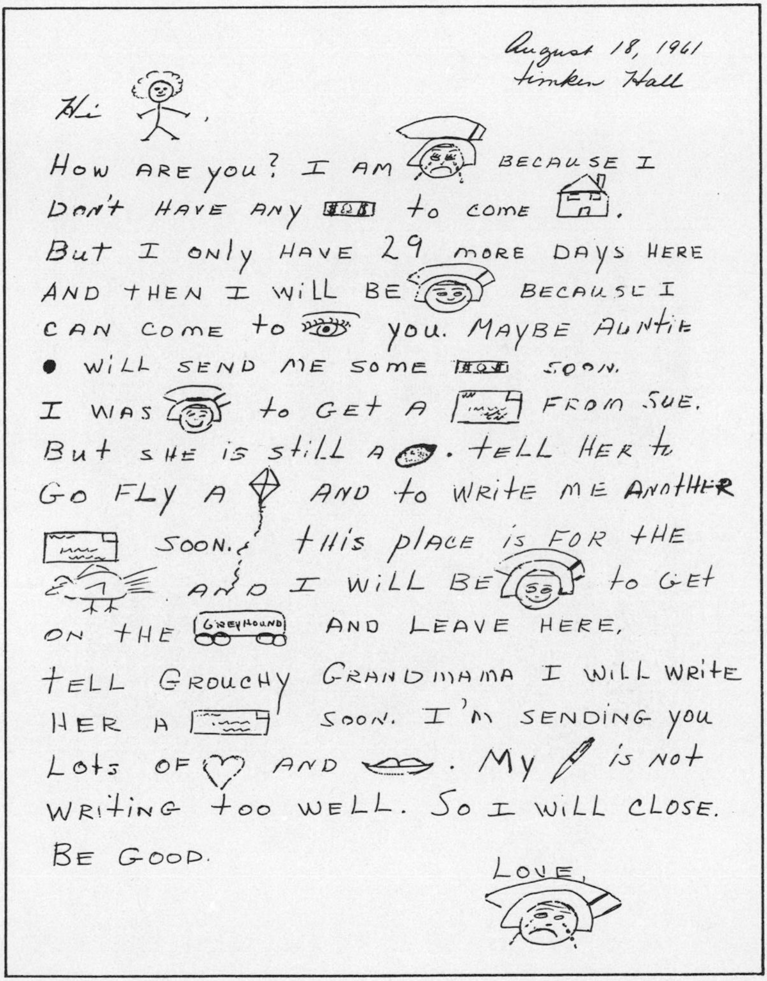

August 18, 1961
Timken Hall

Hi ,

How are you? I am because I don't have any to come . But I only have 29 more days here and then I will be because I can come to you. Maybe Auntie will send me some soon. I was to get a from Sue. But she is still a . tell her to go fly a and to write me another soon. this place is for the and I will be to get on the GREYHOUND and leave here. tell Grouchy Grandmama I will write her a soon. I'm sending you lots of and . My is not writing too well. So I will close. Be good.

Love,